Ghost Hunting Glaciers

Also by Michael Garrigan:

River, Amen

Robbing the Pillars

What I Know [How to Do]

co-written with Andrew Jones,
Songenizios: Poems Inspired by Songs

Ghost Hunting Glaciers

poems

Michael Garrigan

GRAYSON BOOKS
West Hartford, Connecticut
graysonbooks.com

Ghost Hunting Glaciers
Copyright © 2026 by Michael Garrigan
Published by Grayson Books
West Hartford, Connecticut
ISBN: 979-8-9985883-3-4
Library of Congress Control Number: 2025950858

Book and Cover Design by Cindy Stewart
Cover artwork by Elliott Green, "Fictitious Ridge"
Author photo by Jessica Garrigan

For Jessica, Franny, & Whitman

man becomes food for the divinity he worships
—Chris Stevens, Northern Exposure

and the opossum knows his own mind more than I do
—Willi Carlisle

Contents

Landscape Fugue (Spring)

Ferns unfurl from selves hidden in spores, breaking
through frozen soil and the cold that held them in taut
silence. A glancing winter dream of silent stalks and thin
shadows slowly awakens into Mayapple groves spreading

down steep slopes. Fungus cradles algae, leaf brushes leaf,
the intimacy of living is learned again. The slate-blue plumage
of a belted kingfisher plunges into rushing water; her sharp bill
scatters stones into the current, swimming, as it pierces a parr.

Black Bear Confronts Her Conjurer

You dream me for years until one morning

you find me perched on the edge of a ditch

along a gravel road in your waking

as you're walking out of Dugan Run

certain that I am the one you dreamt;

but if you dreamt me, then you must have also dreamt of the endless

Kittatinny Ridge where my eyes first opened one winter

in a soft thicket of twig and breath and hard-darkness.

You must have dreamt of those first berries that my mother

fed me and how they snapped between my teeth,

their sweet tartness filling my mouth with my first taste.

You must have dreamt her, and her quick death.

You conjurer of death, you conjurer of berries, you

conjurer of sharp coldness, stony crevices, brambled tears.

In your greed you dreamt so many of us that I had to leave my home

and follow the ridge until my paws touched asphalt and found a thin

swath of woods that took me to a place of crossing.

The river you conjured I had to swim after waiting three nights as the moon grew to its largest light so I could see where

the grass leaned into the surface and where rock reflected so I knew

where I could rest because I could not see the far bank—you

must have been sleeping so deeply to dream a river this wide—

and once the moon was over the bridge

I stepped into the water and it was cold

even this late in the summer when darkness is short and quick.

I gasped and my lungs filled with air and I dove and for a moment

I wasn't born but floating inside my mother and you were not sleeping

but suspended in this warmth with me.

I held us there for as long as possible;

the current pulled me away into the shallows of an island,

rolling me over and my stomach shivered dry.

The hunger left and I lifted my face

out of water and woke

in the middle of a river and lay still in grass

that moved like eels as clouds drifted apart.

In that moonlight I unfurled and began swimming

and you opened your eyes as I climbed

out at the mouth of a creek and found a path lined with berries

    that I followed to the high ledge where I slept for days.

One morning I smelled you and knew where you'd walk

    because I knew how you dreamt

so I sat waiting here to tell you:

        Dreamer, conjure

a birth that is not a way into death

    and a death that is a way through life

and a love that guides us across the wide river.

Dead Elk Wakes

with a body made of mist

      formed by air pressed by this ravine

            and the sound of the woods he blundered out of:

wolves. thunder. spruce bark sloughing off a bear's claws.
chipmunks in aspen thickets. horseflies on mule deer necks.

                He breathes with wildflower lungs

      He steps like a thawed river worn smooth by sun

          —stone toes and alder leaf eyes
          pine needle fur and larch antlers—

He billows in the breeze of a barred owl skimming dusk

Origins According to Stone Swimmer

I'm lost in wide waves,
echoes of a long-ago collision,
trying to trace a bear's stride.

I come to a place where creeks
meet and a long boulder ledge heaves,
hovering, so I stop. I must. I wait.

Something holds me here;
I listen and watch shadows sickle
through the thick canopy.

There was a winter she slept here.
There was a snow that silenced even her
loud dreams with its quiet gathering.

There was a spring she ate
every berry along this crest;
the streams ran purple.

There was a summer she forgot
about this place and roamed so far
she almost forgot her home.

There was a fall she suckled
under this maple leaf viburnum,
dipping her paws into this thin runnel,

the same water I drink from now.
Look at us, sharing this space, look at us—
one following the other, one leading the other.

I am a stone swimmer, steadily kicking and paddling
my way up these coarse ripples of the Kittatinny Ridge,
balancing on each crease, searching for this dreaming bear.

Epistemology: Seals in Fog

The fog holds so much: salt from sea, gnarled spruce
silhouettes, long lows and muted rumbles, her brother.

Sometimes she hears things she knows are there but never sees.
Hauntings, she thinks. Memories, somewhat. Yearnings, yes.

She finally makes it to the rocks and the ocean is there
as she knew it would be, a trust she follows out to slick

rock where she stands and watches waves of seaweed slide
back & forth in a thick tidal language like a spoon in oatmeal

which the harbor seals swoop through, pump-faking & crossover
dribbling each other like she and her brother used to do playing

one-on-one late into summer nights under gauzy-with-mayfly
floodlights and *Mellon Collie and the Infinite Sadness* playing

on their boombox. They'd take turns switching CDs between
Dawn and Dusk; she adored the lushness of disc two and "1979"

and how "Thirty-Three" sounded like a country harp song
and her brother dug the loud grit of disc one and "Muzzle."

Their bodies move with such abandon childhood ease, skin
muscling skin sticky with Pop-ice sweat & she's about to sink

a three pointer to win as one breaks the surface and claps
so loud she startles awake from that fog back into another.

Dead Elk Considers the Fog

and thinks of his mother who nudged his stomach with Her
nose whenever he stumbled finding a four-legged balance.

> She smelled of sticky pine.
> Her breath was always hot.
> She bit ticks off his back.

When he fell through a thicket of brambles
She used her teeth to pluck thorns from his face.

When he fell through the ice She bit the fat
of his neck and pulled him to dry ground.

Today it is fog, tomorrow, another
memory of a mouth mothering
until his antlers drop.

Dead Elk Wonders Where His Body Is

The light that is not from here
sometimes crawls across ridges
and busies itself all night
never reaching that far
but always catching
always demanding.

One morning he woke without muscle
and an itch behind where his ear would be
and realized that he had stared at those lights
for too long, that he had become just something
chasing something else, that he no longer knew
what it felt like for his soles to sink into soil.

Vernal Pool Self Portraits of Black Bear

I lope into every vernal pool

      I see scattering salamanders and let my body

sink in the spiraling galaxy of gelatinous wood frog

      eggs mirroring all the life that has rivered

through me, rippling in a Pollocked universe with no

      gravity, careening and splattering into a frenzied

kaleidoscope as I watch infinite lives

      stretching and twirling and colliding

until I see my mother float by on the wings of an osprey

      and she smiles at my father

hanging from an ouzel's foot and a beetle boring

      itself into the bark of a pine my mother,

as a cub, climbed as wolves chased her that,

      years later, dried from the inside out and fell

and became the den I was born in; the seed it grew

      from catches in my eyelid and I trace

threads of soil and needle and bark as water

and cells and lignin of that little piñon

eddy billow and flutter and break open into me.

23

Epistemology: Bullfrogs

She once hiked to the mouth of a creek and,
since it was a wet spring, found a vernal pool

just off the main river full of bullfrogs courting
and mating, some latched on the back of others,

some full-throated searching, yearning, expanding
and contracting into questions and answers.

Translucent tendrils, like roots, curled
through the pool, dark pods in their centers.

She knelt, knees wet, and sunk into pebbles, nose to water,
staring at black circles waiting for tails to emerge. Tonight,

she's falling asleep to their chorus in the old canal
loving more and more that silence between each call.

Dead Elk Hears the Soundtrack to His Biopic Starring Woody Harrelson

every time he chews on clusters of Indian paintbrush.

It must be the color coating his lips that gets him into character, that
starts him strutting through larch, swaying his haunches, stretching his
chest, flaring his nostrils, rubbing his pointed, obtuse rack on everything
it leans into making sure the eagles see it through the canopy, letting sun
catch it; *no one will fuck with me* he mutters and the music of his
swagger across the duff crescendos right as he reaches water and the
river takes his lit Camel light and he drinks and his lips are washed
clean and he hears nothing in the sunset as the stars slowly start
scrolling through the credits.

River According to Stone Swimmer

I float in the heaviness of a hard body
needing to cross every river I come to.
Sometimes I wrestle with Bear as we;

sometimes I dive with a hungry Osprey,
hunting for anything that swims upstream,
holding form in an upswell of warm air as we;

sometimes I swim in the wake of a Woman's long
stroke, sipping every ripple, hatching her questions
into mayflies swarming lights, darkening skies as we;

sometimes I become so slick Crayfish think
I am quick current and we swim backwards,
stripping open the thin spathe between worlds as we

push up and pull away and tumble
against and tangle towards and rest within
and dream each other into existence.

Iridescent Nostalgia of Black Bear

I climb the long rock spine

    that was once so high off the river

when wind whipped upstream whitecaps

    looked like distant snow-covered peaks,

but now, with dams arresting the current,

    I'm close enough to see below the surface

where, once the serviceberries turned white, shad

    ran and all I'd have to do was scoop my paw

as if I was cupping ants out of a dead chestnut

    to hold something shimmering; now it's just

catfish. My teeth have grown dull and soft without

    munching on those silver incandescent flakes.

I'd swallow the sea and my whole body bloomed,

    radiating purple and pink chrome as I became

sun for all the trillium and geranium. I still shine,

    eating a cormorant egg each spring.

Dead Elk Swims with Bull Trout

in the stillness that holds

    the river into a quiet dark,

he watches colors he knows from the moon

    —an embrace, a mirror—

he sees himself for the first time without eyes,
bone only, and in the skull-white refraction
of mottled light he finally breathes water,
nosing into the underside of a large boulder
that's never not known wetness; he comes
nose to nose jaw to jaw with Bull Trout
who lingers long enough to ride the currents
frictionless, upstream, softening as they slalom
against stone making the river bottom a path
home holding every color of every memory.

Glacier Triptych According to Stone Swimmer

1.

Black sand rubs
against the edges
of thin frozen

shelves as waves
lunge towards land
over and over

2.

Where I stand
collision is just
constant creations of

water embracing water,
white-crowned sparrows
singing through hail

3.

Black bear knows
how melt tastes—
a quick sweetness

and salty deadwood.
Tracing her tracks,
I unbury memory.

Epistemology: Fishing the Sulphur Hatch on the Little Juniata River, She Thinks of How Easy it is to Tell Someone She Loves Them

and yet it's usually only when light is about to leave that she reaches
to the surface, breaking soft currents, to reveal what she hungers for.

Dead Elk Eats a Rhododendron Bloom and Accidentally Has a Psychedelic Experience

He tucks himself into a hillside of blooming rhododendron waiting for the heat to cool, watching hawk shadows careen across the ravine and through his daydreams. After a few hours, he can no longer resist their scarlet brightness and wonders if they taste like Swedish Fish and would stick to his molars so he touches the flowers to his lips and nibbles and chews and swallows and stares for a few minutes. It tastes of salty almonds and diesel chocolate and meadow tea slushies. The wind stops. The light filtering through spruce shutters and camera clicks and he's a Polaroid picture flicked and snapped until a form slowly shapes the white space of hunger and awe as his face peels like September birch bark and his eyes crackle like hemlock needles touched to flame and the stream below him turns to mad honey that he's tumbling towards, delving into, letting it take him away. He floats like a stone finally lifted from its resting spot and thinks he's free, rolling and balancing and riding the wave towards its natural crest, until he realizes that even when you're dead you're held by the land that's always been there, murmuring; so he licks and slurps the sweet river until he's sweetened and caramelized and he swims on the gratitude of being full once again and gazes back up the hillside to see the daughter they had only known for one year before losing her to the wanderings—her eyes were his, her smell was her mother's. He tries to ask her where she lived and who she cared for and tell her a joke about elephants to hear her laugh, but all that comes out is a five piece free jazz song careening against boulders into a deep processional cacophony of backwater and bullfrogs and by the time the piano and trumpet and saxophone and drum and bass die the wings he never knew she had, that he never knew were possible, swoop her away. He cries until he remembers her mother who he loved and looked for each fall and he drifts in their shared warmth which, like all passion, pulls him to the surface of the moment as he washes up onto an island of driftwood and thrush song trickles through his jaw and the canopy opens into a cedar lined symphony hall and his lungs are lichen and the clouds breathe in and breathe out with him as he lies there until all the light leaves the trees and he feels the hardness of gravity; now, he looks

for them in every flowering bloom knowing they are the firmament he
will always exist within.

II

Landscape Fugue (Summer)

Owls swoop across the night, coughing up pellets. Box turtle,
black bears, and white-footed mice sow Mayapple seeds
through thicket and thunder; the matted soil where they sleep
soundly through thick cricket hum and hare thumping becomes

green umbrella clusters next spring. A waxing half-
moon cannot reach the tiny trumpet cup lichen bending
from rotting hickory; here's how our world spreads—
stretching into a deep exhale, rooting in small breaths.

Long Plateaus of Black Bear

When ice has melted but there is still

    snow in the crooks that barely see sun,

I find switchbacks bighorn sheep have threaded

    through morels and silverweed and walk

until my sides are scratched by thistle and stung by nettle

    not minding any of these heats because I know

where I'm going is always cool; up and up and up

    I plod and meander and the air lightens

and the dew on my hips dries and my berry-stained fur

    crisps and I lick last night's storms

off spruce cones I find lying along the trail;

    I begin to hum a song that has been sung

since before I was born, since before I left

    my home range, since before, when these valleys

were oceans and everything swam and water was their air;

    and this song takes me above tree line

and onto a long bald plateau where I sit and watch

    the mountains that have been home until my

eyes blur and the ridges reach into the past on one side

    and the future on the other and the present

is an infinite sky in front of me and I am able to see

    how some of this has been created by collision

and upheaval and some of it has been sculpted

    by slowly receding glaciers and erosion

and my wonder bursts into awe of how little of life

    has anything to do with things

I've done or thought or felt and so much to do

    with what has been laid out by others.

Dead Elk Finds His Body

in the spindrift mist of water hitting rock,
lying still, skin saturated, fur peeled off,
his skull catching a little moonlight
his ribs long gone, nothing left
of his jowls that used to sway
when he stalked through
these woods knowing
each root ball
so well

and wonders what he ever did
with just four legs and two eyes
  and how much life he missed
  and how much love he lost
not able to walk further and see clearer
under the muscled weight of living

Dead Elk Lies Down Under a Sunset

Light glances off his few remaining
tufts of fur and flutters into a whisper
hushing down the ridge towards tree line.

Mosquito heat swells as he succumbs to red; flickering
in his eye cavity memories of magpies and joy and soothing.
What has he given? What has he eased for something else?

Now, everything. His bones hold the day-end purple
light and radiates it throughout the no-moon night
for wolves and owls hunting our world as we sleep.

Epistemology: Conejohela Flats

She knows this mud and how it collapses
around her ankles and folds over her toes
and holds her thighs and swallows her sandals.

The marsh wren watches her drag the kayak
through shallow water lifting her legs like a heron,
hoping she'll stop sinking before she's stuck.

She sits on a sycamore and watches the river flatten,
listening to the Green-winged Teals and Terns scrabble
through shrubs and bindweed, tracing her line through lotus.

She pours out her coffee and pushes into current swinging her
downstream, lightly kissing the river with paddles, and floats
slower than clouds, trying to name each bird she sees.

She's never been able to figure out what "Conejohela" means
and if the "j" is soft like an "h" or hard like deadwood stacked
in the muddy flats. She says it with a "j," offering structure.

But she knows that in spring eel grass are dark spots and by June
they sway together in green and by August they're so thick they
turn the river into wet moss that she can barely paddle through.

Names are like that sometimes—thin water and thick mud;
She sounds them slowly, tracing each letter with her tongue.

Larkspur According to Stone Swimmer

Purple cups, buttery in the summer sun,
keep me company and hold the grief of spent
red trillium. It's too hot to be here, but I'm here

anyway knowing she lumbers in the high hills;
humidity slows us down. I know her only by dry
scat; I am following her days-ago-meanderings

content with these wildflowers and long days keeping
us awake, our vision bursting with blooms shimmering
as quick as tufted titmouse calls shuffling through redbuds.

Dead Elk Drifts

and thinks of sinking

    his teeth into a rotten

apple from that tree seeded

    after a hard winter

so its roots know what frozen

    ground feels like

and those apples hold that knowing

    of how to live after a

long death like he holds this river

    like larch hold his liver red

antler velvet until snow pulls it to dirt

Forgotten Peaks of Black Bear

There are mountains I have shown you

      that you refuse to remember.

What else am I to do?

      So much of kindness is noticing.

I mosey over a long brim of scrub

      into a basin of three alpine lakes

plucking my way to contentment.

Reading According to Stone Swimmer

After every rain I drift down gravel roads
until I find ferns that say something worth
hearing and trample through them without

knowing exactly where I'm going. I stand
on stones small enough to hold me and look
down into mud, beyond the wild geraniums,

searching for prints to trace. Pink flowers
are commas that ask me to pause, so I do,
until I find a long run-on of split beechnuts

punctuated by short acorn fragments
and I watch as her story unfolds in rotten
logs and vernal ponds full of throaty frogs.

Dead Elk Smells Fire

in his sleep and snorts into his blanket

        of moss

creating a cowlick of fur and needle

        sap;

he walks to the ledge

        and stands behind a rock,

stilled,

        hoping for thunder,

looking for his father whose scent

        always settles on every green

thing when it rains; it's getting harder

        to remember, to notice,

to wait for fire to turn hardness to soft ash,

        wondering if anyone still smells him.

Epistemology: Gut Road

It was always 2Pac's *Makaveli* in the tape deck
stuck clicking back and forth every six songs.

They'd get through both sides at least twice
before even thinking about starting the car.

Sometimes the beat pulsed with the current eddying along the island
& thin ceiling fabric swaying down, smoke folding out the windows.

Even now she doesn't know a single word of any of the songs,
but she knows how sunlight nestled in each ring of the culvert

and how their conversations washed out of it even in drought
with the war cry of a blue jay always hanging at its mouth.

At her grandmother's house just up the road she'd watch
robins fight blue jays trying to steal their eggs and marvel

at their relentless pursuit of the yolk of another. She
liked it when their hands just settled on their thighs.

He drove the road without catching any of the axle-busting potholes &
she fell in love with how he floated the LeSabre over the washboards.

She could, & still does, name every plant that grew between them
& the river & wonders if he still knows all the lyrics she never learned.

Back then the world, even the rutted-out parts, seemed smooth, easy.
Back then she listened to albums she didn't like four times in a row.

Raid Peak According to Stone Swimmer

Every place has a valley just over its crest
few venture into. Most people only follow the trails,
turning back as they end, relying only on sight.

Follow water to its root, climb towards the horizon
until Raid Peak punctures it. Wander and amble
back and forth down the steep topography towards

the base of the mountain. There, look up, trace
the alpine blood clot lichen and seams of gneiss
until you find us on the ridge, tumbling into sky.

Dead Elk Finally Swims in the Ocean

How he found all this sand he'll never know,

     but this, he does: all lakes were once oceans

and all oceans will become something he'll

     slowly circumambulate and know intimately.

For now, he likes how these trunks fit so he

     pounces into a wave yelping with salty lips

as dark-eyed juncos paddle him out to deep water.

Soil Songs of Black Bear

I sing between storms

    as sun dissolves clouds

and light refracts off water

    and I see the world kaleidoscopically,

when my vocal chords have warmed

    and my paws are covered in drying mud.

I lick them slowly and begin my song,

    which is never the same because soil

always tastes differently; sometimes

    it's a loamy blues song, sometimes

it's a peaty jazz melody, sometimes

    it's a slick silty plucked bluegrass tune.

I suck on hail to sweeten the rhythm

    and the lyrics come in a single letter

of a single word of a single sentence

    holding the story of every stone.

When mountains begin to write

    the rain and slope wind brings

the breath of the becomer, I lick my paws clean

and ease into silence, listening

as red-eyed vireos and white-crowned sparrows

lilt into a symphony of deep woods.

Dead Elk Antlers a Constellation

The sky is so dark he can't see

    the red cedar or the puff balls stemming

from soft birch as he steps into spore plumes

    that settle on his ulna and tibia and tarsal.

Awake, willing to walk into that darkness,

    but tired of not treading lightly, carefully,

he arches his atlas and axis and cervical, sweeping

    his antlers across his legs in a perfect balancing act

of grace, agility, and certainty, swinging those bones

    he's stood on his whole life into the air,

spinning and scattering them across that endless blank

    slate his mother wrote their stories on;

lying on the ground, he watches them

    reach escape velocity, becoming stars

and constellations planted with this final upright act;

    little lights keeping us from trampling our tenderness.

III

Landscape Fugue (Autumn)

Nothing sleeps soundly during an autumn drought
with leaves crisp on branches; every tiny breeze
every squirrel stepping every tufted titmouse picking
through clutter for seed cracks the straining tautness.

Columbine seeds split open from their tense pods,
straining against a long sleep. Larch struck in monk's
hood glance their golden light against dying ferns
finally resting on soil that will feed their next form.

Old Oceans of Black Bear

1.

Something's always following me

      and I've chosen to let it

instead of always looking back;

      if it finds me, I have found myself.

2.

I find enough red elderberry to stain

      my whole body with its juice each June.

In September, I squint through slender

      tamarack thistles for every shade of red

as the last snow-in-summer is covered with needles,

      my mouth still thick with sweet syrup.

3.

Someday I will doze off in a field of full sun

      until my darkness glasses over

like deep inland lakes at dawn and slowly

      swim in the old oceans of my teeth

towards islands of wood lilies and holly fern

until whatever it is that's following me

finds me so we can tread together

in the abundance of our shared lives.

Dead Elk Snores

and no one hears his breaths
rattle bone, no one wakes him
                              to roll him
over.

No one sees his misty eyelashes
twitch in the dark when he dreams
of crickets and tall grass and how
he and his sister would lie down,
surrounded, hidden from heat.

In the mornings after he doesn't dream,
                        he cannot eat
and instead lives inside his hunger
        that is no longer just in his stomach
                but is now all of him;
like a ligament threading through
        his scapula up to his mandible,
he jaws at the air that smells
        of memories sinewing and is never full
knowing that dying isn't always a death,
that sometimes it's just a yearning
        for what nourishes

Dead Elk Stares

until something moves

                    that he cannot name.

When he was young,
when he followed
his mother and slept
in the cradle of her legs and stomach
and the grass was a dark green,
always wet, even after the sun
had reached as far as it could reach
and to touch her fur was to touch
a crackling stalk,

        he knew no words

                for this world

                    and loved it without

                          language.

His eyes finally move, dry, caught
in the wind as it lifts an eagle
across the river, searching, knowing
the only way to love is without words.

Epistemology: Rain

Only after getting wet does she ever realize it's raining;
even obvious storm clouds & thunder can't ruin the surprise.

One time a cricket jumped off the tip of tall grass where she was
watching it balance and landed on her arm, just below the blue jay

tattoo on her wrist. She watched as it read her world with its antennae,
smelling and seeing her with its palps, always searching, never stilling.

She wondered what would make her become quiet long enough
to settle—a handful of grapes? how his hands cradled and crawled

up & down the maple ebony of his stand-up bass? a mourning dove
being stalked by a cat?—Until she realized she was staring long

after the cricket had jumped back into the field. It was raining;
each drop a full stop, a held stillness until it touched something else.

Wind According to Stone Swimmer

Wind will always be the way
my world is seen; I trace her
scent on each pebble of hail.

Dead Elk Saunters through a Reclaimed Strip Mine

Dirt roads sieve mounds of thistle and macadam where mountains of coal once held his family's home; now, grazing brown scratches of land are herds relocated here with names he does not know, so he just gazes and itches and wonders until he sees one with antlers that look like his brother's—their arches and how they curve, their points and how they pierce, their balance and how they posture him into an uprightness even as he lies in dry switchgrass—that makes him think of his first pair and how he couldn't hold their weight. He looked at the world crookedly, constantly nodding left and right, everything slanted and sloped; he knocked them against every branch and pine cone until a pair of woodcocks nested in the crook of his only tine, somehow thinking he was the ground; perhaps because he walked so slowly; perhaps because they knew his adolescence was a shelter of safety; perhaps they were lost like he was. His antlers kept pulling his body towards desire, away from contentment, and he didn't notice the eggs hatched until one morning there was a nasally *peent* behind his ear. When he stopped digging his self-anointing hole he finally, actually, listened, and heard the sticky softness coming from the nest he'd been awkwardly cradling. He began to walk slower, more deliberately, and to watch their parents doodle around the timber for food; he gathered so many seeds in every joint and tucked along his ribs he could barely bend and when he breathed and sauntered he felt the small hard hope of life scratching into him. As they ate and grew they became louder and his world was filled with buzzing trills for a whole season as he finally found balance and could walk without tripping. Long after they left for more warmth and the nest fell with his antlers into early spring snow at the base of an oak, he still heard the melodies they taught him; now, with wind sleeving through his joints, huffing air through his large nostril crevices, he spreads wildflower and apple and chestnut and persimmon seeds across stripped soil so next year there will be more twittering and whirring and cricketing and clacketing and chirping and maybe these herds will hear his family name in that nourishing rupture of noise and bugle the songs still echoing along his spine.

Found Postcard of Black Bear

I'm doing well and seeing so much.

    I miss you and our den, I miss

our mornings, I miss how we tumble

    down dead trails, I miss the wildflower

crown you placed on me at the lake of our first date;

    someday I'll come home.

Last night I had the most amazing dinner

    of honeyed stonecrop leaves dappled with ants.

Remember that night we had in the briars?

    I was reminded of that this morning,

waking with a sore body, knowing

    muscles I had never known.

Bird Song According to Stone Swimmer

When it's all I can hear
        I'm reminded of how eels love,
                without the world knowing.

I choose the way of the birds
        letting everything see the joy of waking,
                of feeding one another, of the sun.

In moments when the woods are quiet,
        I think about succession and how lightning
                bugs only exist when they blink in the dark;

I grow into a field of ferns
        waiting for a breeze to rustle
                my softness and reveal hidden nettles;

I think about elk once gathering and dipping
        across these mountains and how their bugles
                must have sounded against hard chestnut,

how so much fed on that fruit hidden in spiny
        burs until first frost, how so much shade was given
                to sweltering life, how listening is an act of love.

Dead Elk Attends a Billy Strings Concert

Reckless ain't even the word;
      surrounded in the pit by all this skin and meat
         reminds him of his first winter,
         how they kept warm by curling close.
   All nuzzle,
       all plucked lip,
           all eyebrow in armpit,
all soft chest strums against hard bellies;

   Deliberate picks, ragged harmonies;
   For months they were just one itchy *thing*.

Their bodies bend & break around each other,
moving like they're tumbling through rapids.
     Free, would be the word.
         Limber, another.
            Together, also.

All this movement must be intimacy, he thinks.
All the bodies absorb the sound and he remembers
a grove of pines his mother took he and his sister
to right before she was about to give the world
more of herself and there was a feeling there he had never felt,
as if once they stepped into the circle of trees the needles grew
like roots wrapping around their ankles and their mother
told them not to move and not to be scared, just to be held
by this world for a while because now they were
part of some song they'd always be humming
without ever knowing all the words.

As the stage empties he leans over
     whispering tie dye into the nearest neck
         reminding them to put his body back
         under pine-soil when the music ends.

Epistemology: Estuary

A melding stillness—
her feet sunken firm in this small
estuary where creek meets ocean;

seaweed and small stones painted with root blood,
creeping dogwood in sand around her ankles, spruce
holding wind even when water is flat calm at her back.

She watches brook trout coast in on high tide
chased by some larger fish—stripers maybe?
would they eat something so beautiful? —

and marvels at how they hold the soft color of salt
around each faint halo and how their skin maps tides
and currents and how one mineral can change a body.

Soft Churches of Black Bear

Parry's primrose, bluegill,

      cicada buzzing through a thunderstorm,

stone swimming down slope towards the river,

      brook trout darting under a cutbank

as a fisher bounds and leaps from above,

      a fox that prances along a fallen

locust straddling a stream where I once

      watched a woman nap all day

crouched across from her

      in a thicket of mountain laurel;

I tried to see her dreams, which

      never happens, so I breathed

with her and when she woke and took her pack

      and walked off into the woods, I sat

in her scent until wind came and my belly growled.

      I scratch underneath my legs when I'm tired.

I watch fog lift and marvel at how it lingers. I wait.

Dead Elk Speaks His Mother's Name

and the fog

lifts.

Lake According to Stone Swimmer

Pike have brushed against me
        as I have spent centuries
watching water shelf against rock.

My stillness is just a myth,
        as is the hummingbird's,
as is the rattling shush of quaking aspen.

Just wait for any wind
        and you'll finally see
me; in this caesura is where we meet

traveling through each other's dreams,
        though only with the patience
of a lake will we wake to another's presence.

Epistemology: Skinny Dipping at 10,500 Feet

She's never known a cold as cold
      as slowly wading into a tarn of snow
melt; shattering, enveloping, breathless.
      Always refusing the quickness
that jumping would offer;
      the all-encompassing shutter
before calm buoyancy of acclimation,
      she chooses to step slowly,
inching forward, letting her whole body
      feel and respond, each shiver
just another reason to keep going,
      another reason to stare at the glow
along the bare ridge, another reason
      to focus on the boulder further out
and consider how it will look in the winter
      surrounded by ice and snow,
how it will feel much like how she felt
      in her sleeping bag last night,
tossing and turning as the tent frosted over,
      some part of her skin always restless,
tight, constricted by the cold and how
      that wasn't a choice, just misfortune;
but this water, this lake, is a choice,
      so she chooses to take
another step and another deep breath
      and the sun shimmers off
the wind gliding across the surface
      and the brightness warms
her enough that she finally pushes
      forward and submerges her
head and feels a companionship
      between herself sand this place,
as if they were always mingling,
      and the languages of her heart

and body finally speak in concert
         as she comes up for air.

Dead Elk Sleeps Next to a Decommissioned
Nuclear Power Plant

and still hears the thrum of the turbines
and smells strontium-90 in hot-cell ghosts
and still tastes uranium on blueberry leaves.

The morning glow reminds him
of the time their forest burned
and he ran down valley with wolves
        and the hares
                and the mule deer
                        and the hawks
        cut through ash clouds
mapping their way to safety,

but they lost each other in the smoke,
he and his mother and his sister split
like atoms by the collision of ember and
fur; he felt his sister burn, her leg caught
between a boulder and a pile of still-hard dead
cedar, and when the air cleared he found his mother
and they stepped into water to cool their hooves and
began the waiting that is always there, stored, humming.

IV

Landscape Fugue (Winter)

Light as crisp as a grackle's call grazes a still
lake warming nothing; snow cradles Ambush Peak.
Wildflowers once caught this light, but now
just granite brushed with moon and Jewel lichen.

Frozen water settles sighs and cracks like aspen
from a hidden spring of heat under a clutch of moss.
Cedar cones hold limbs stretched over soil softly woven
by fern rhizomes and stitched with lupine seeds, waiting.

Life Goals of Black Bear

When I was a cub, I wished to eat

      as many blackberries as I could find.

When I was older, all I wanted was a den

      tucked into a hillside and someone in spring

to share all that rain with. Now, I try to live like

      lichen—two becoming one—

but it's hard knowing what the other needs.

      I have a creek I go to when trees drop

their leaves and the surface is like a carving

      of the seasons we have just lived.

I sip, I drink, I dip my whole body into it

      and as I submerge in the fallen

I finally sense more than this body has ever sensed;

      the habitat I thought I was balancing

on the palm of my paw presses against my muscles

      and bones and makes me heavy until

I am weightless, floating within the existence of every

      small thing that has ever made this place.

Dead Elk Drops His Antlers

it is so easy to lift your head and look up
without the weight of the need to be seen.

Snowline According to Stone Swimmer

There's not much snow anymore along
our loping ridges, but when we're blessed
with a few Nor'easters and weeks of freeze

I know I'll be able to follow the receding
snowline and get close to her faint trails;
in the slow thaw is where we almost touch.

We reach for that migrating melt,
reading its cursive shadows on stone,
spending the spring ghost hunting glaciers.

Epistemology: Parking Lot Muskies

When the river floods the boat ramps
and parking lots become backwater eddies,
she walks down to watch him stand ankle
deep in his muck boots casting giant flies—

feathers layered on seven-inch shanks that
come from some rainbow mottled barnyard—
looking for a musky roaming into the macadam shallows
gorging on bait fish with all that turbid tumult at its back.

She's seen him hook two and land one. Both times
they yelled together right at the teeth-on-fly moment
when the world seized and all air left all lungs and a fierce
violence of water they never speak of again overtook them.

The one he lost snapped off as he reached
for it and she stared as he stood in a still sigh,
silent, line curled, gazing out into muddy foam.

The other he cradled in water, holding all that predation
knowing it could tear him at any moment, memorizing each
dark flank-stripe to trace while he casts endlessly into currents;

bowing to the river and all it held, he whispered to that thin
space between its eyes and she finally understood devotion.

Dead Elk Listens to the Last Crickets

and understands what's done and what's to come.

He sighs into the hillside
and for the whole length of that breath
he is simply hard ground—

                      he knows nothing;
                he is an ocean of sediment,

      a universe of needled soil
      a handful of slim fir seeds
      a horse fly with heavy wings
      a hovering whorl of Jo-Pye
      a shard of broken plastic
      a shoelace tied to a stick
      a shiny Hershey's Kiss wrapper—

then another breath and he's back to listening.

Winter Dens of Black Bear

I search for months

     until I find a cedar hugged

granite boulder eaving a warm

     hollow cupping dry ground

and drag pine boughs and moss clumps

     deep into the softest, coolest

nook of the cavity before snow gathers

     in ragged clusters along the edge

of the longest branches. Sometimes I wake

     in a restlessness of wind through wheat

and lick roots to taste the leaves and sun and spicy

     scent, shadows of summer I bask in

until I fall asleep spooning a stone

     worn smooth from all my dreams.

Epistemology: Little Loves

This morning she woke to her dog
snoring in her armpit. She fell back to sleep.

She wakes again to him
rustling around the kitchen,

making dough and something sweet
and lies there for a bit, just listening,

on the last day of the year, in wonder
with how she got here, in all this warmth,

forgiving herself for all the little moments of pushing
back on what the world was offering, all those little loves,

and just now she peels an orange and reheats the last
cinnamon bun for an afternoon snack that balances

sweet and tart just right before walking the dogs along the river
in what she imagines will be a sunset she refuses to look away from.

Memory According to Stone Swimmer

I live in glacial memories.
These oceans are the first,
then peaks and ridges unfold

as streams and valleys tumble and ease,
rush and meander, towards rivers and bays,
all returning to the echo of our beginning.

Dead Elk Scratches a Tree into a Ghazal

He first sees the tree as a sapling in spring,
its needle tufts softly reaching, learning to sing.

In the summer of its sixth year, a larch branch breaks
and falls against its side, scraping leaning pressing.

That winter, he grows tired of all the searching
so he curls into the warmth of his legs digging.

When he wants to mate, tired of being alone,
he finds a tree big enough to hold his etchings

and all fall he itches his antlers, scratching
and rubbing, bone against bark, exposing.

To drink is to dip his bare song makers into the river
and he shakes them dry as the air turns into a blessing.

The wolves learn of him by his hoof prints and musk;
they fall on him once he grows tired of all the chasing.

In his last breaths he hears his voice from the etched tree rising
through rivering needles into a name the bark will always sing.

Dead Elk Thinks His Last Thoughts & Speaks His Last Words

sun on ridge purple moonlight mother's breath
rivers speaking rocks hearing alders hugging
morning grunts breaking frost thistle sister wolves
snowy hooves glistening pink in a dawn meander

                            become all of this

Love According to Stone Swimmer

It is a den of seed and stick.
When one of us moves, the other
leafs into the other like twirling pollen.

It is a caddis lifting off a stream
in mid-afternoon, a mourning dove cooing
in the evening, a barred owl hooting at night;

it is the rust I scratch against in the shed,
it is the dog nuzzling me when no one
else sees me; it is the way boulders settle,

treading in an eternal moment;
the way a bicycle collapses time,
the way elk refuse to die.

I have known it in every
moment and yet I seek it,
refusing to believe it ends.

Black Bear Dreams of Elk

It is easy to dream

    in the shade of mayapples.

Here, so close to ground, I smell

    everything. White oak, pine;

hickory nuts and acorns; enough to live

    in either world. When leaves,

smudged yellow-white, crumble into a den,

    I sleep on memory of meals

eaten along a creek with a bottom so sandy

    all I have to do is nuzzle its surface

to drink that soft grit. I scrape it against my teeth

    and conjure an Elk. I watch all winter

as he lives each season; I listen with ears covered

    by lobed leaves and eyes shut with nut shells.

I wake as wolves take him to the ground

    opening my eyes to a stalkless world.

About the Author

Michael Garrigan writes and teaches along the Susquehanna River in Pennsylvania. He is the author of two previous poetry collections: *River, Amen* (winner of the Weatherford Award for Poetry) and *Robbing the Pillars*. His writing has appeared in *Orion*, *The Flyfish Journal*, *Talking River Review*, *Water~Stone Review*, *Saranac Review*, *The Hopper Magazine*, *River Teeth*, and *North American Review*, among others. His work has been nominated for Best of the Net, Best Small Fictions, Best Spiritual Literature, and The Pushcart Prize. Michael was the Artist in Residence for The Bob Marshall Wilderness Area and believes every watershed should have a Poet Laureate. You can find more of his work at www.mgarrigan.com.

Acknowledgments

I am grateful to the editors of the journals, magazines, websites, and anthologies who published poems from this book, some in slightly different forms or under different titles.

About Place Journal - "Dead Elk Wonders Where His Body Is," "Dead Elk Stares," "Dead Elk Drifts"

Camas Magazine - "Landscape Fugues"

Cider Press Review - "Epistemology: Gut Road"

Cutleaf Journal - "Dead Elk Antlers a Constellation," "Dead Elk Listens to the Last Crickets," "Dead Elk Saunters through a Reclaimed Strip Mine"

The Evergreen Review - "Black Bear Confronts Her Conjuror," "Glacier Triptych According to Stone Swimmer," and "Origins According to Stone Swimmer"

The FlyFish Journal - "Epistemology: Parking Lot Muskies"

The Glacier - "Dead Elk Eats a Rhododendron Bloom and Accidentally Has a Psychedelic Experience," "Lake According to Stone Swimmer"

Mothman Was Here Anthology - "Dead Elk Finds His Body"

Peach Fuzz Magazine - "Epistemology: Little Loves"

Psaltery & Lyre - "Epistemology: Rain"

Quarter Notes Magazine - "Dead Elk Attends a Billy Strings Concert," "Dead Elk Hears the Soundtrack to His Biopic Starring Woody Harrelson"

River Mouth Review - "Epistemology: Bullfrogs"

Saranac Review - "Dead Elk Sleeps Next to a Decommissioned Nuclear Power Plant"

Split Rock Review - "Epistemology: Seals in Fog"

Talking River Review - "Dead Elk Wakes," "Dead Elk Snores"

Terrain - "Bird Song According to Stone Swimmer"

Wayfarer Magazine - "Epistemology: Estuary," "Raid Peak According to Stone Swimmer"

Whale Road Review - "Dead Elk Considers the Fog"

The book's first epigraph is used courtesy of Universal Studios Licensing, LLC.

Notes & Gratitude

The "Landscape Fugues" are inspired by Jeff Parker's music, mainly his *Mondays at The Enfield Tennis Academy* and *Forfolks* records.

Dead Elk arrived on a ledge along the Middlefork of the Flathead River in the Great Bear Wilderness. I was there with the support and kindness of the Bob Marshall Wilderness Foundation, the Flathead National Forest, Swan Valley Connections, and the Hockaday Museum. Thank you for giving me those two weeks in the backcountry and for introducing me to another world.

I extend my deepest thanks to the landscapes and wild places, along with the organizations and people that work to protect them and all our public lands, that greatly influenced this book: Quehanna Wild Area, Dolly Sods Wilderness Area, Bridger Wilderness, Popo Agie Wilderness, Bob Marshall Wilderness, and especially my home, the Lower Susquehanna River Watershed.

Thank you to Ginny Connors and Alberto Ríos for believing in this book and giving it a home.

I am incredibly grateful for the writers and artists who supported and inspired me throughout the writing of these poems: Todd Davis, Noah Davis, Ryan Brod (sorry for missing that pike on the first cast, but it found its way into a poem), Jory Mickelson, Anne Haven McDonnell, Erin Block, Andrew Jones, Corrie Williamson, Grant Clauser, Chris LaTray, Geffrey Davis, Jason Rolfe, and Richard Harrington.

Thank you to Jessica, Franny, and Whitman for creating a home full of love in the woods along the river.